THE DRAWINGS OF
HEINRICH KLEY

THE DRAWINGS OF
HEINRICH KLEY

DOVER PUBLICATIONS, INC.
NEW YORK

CONTENTS

HEINRICH KLEY

In 1908, in the Munich Expressionist literary and art magazine, *Die Jugend,* there suddenly appeared, unheralded and unexpected, a series of remarkable pen and ink sketches signed "Kley." Sometimes black and white, sometimes covered with color washes, usually without captions, they were characterized by a highly individual skittery technique, and a subject matter that leaped wildly about from satire to near-obscenity to despair. They were the first mature works of one of the greatest cartoonists of modern times, Heinrich Kley.

Who was Heinrich Kley? This was a question that was probably asked many times in Munich, for the sketches aroused a great amount of interest. Actually, Kley was one of the last men whom one would have expected to create such fantasies. Before 1908 he had simply been one of many capable academic artists. Born in 1863 in Karlsruhe in the Rhineland, he received his first training in the "practical arts" curriculum of the Karlsruhe Akademie, where he studied under Ferdinand Keller. He later finished his studies under C. Frithjof Smith in Munich. His earliest work, from 1888 to about 1892, consisted of portraits, landscapes, still lifes, city scenes, and historical paintings—mostly unexceptional work. Some of his paintings had found their way into museum collections: "Drinkers," "The Kreutzer Sonata," "In the Boudoir," and so on. He had also been responsible for two historical murals in the post office in Baden Baden: "The Consecration of the Roman Altar to Mercury," and "Kaiser Wilhelm the First's Walk."

Kley had also created for himself a small reputation as a very competent depicter of industrial scenes, which he painted in oils and water color, from about 1892. He gathered his subject matter from the processes of manufacturing, and turned coal and steam and sweat into paintings which showed considerable understanding of the processes involved in industry. His "Pouring Steel at Krupp" had been praised as "catching the poetry of the modern machine world," and George Grosz has recorded his delight with one of Kley's industrial watercolors. Unfortunately, none of these pre-1908 paintings has been reproduced in a form available to the English-speaking world, but if we may judge from descriptions of them, and from the Black Forest landscape which appeared in *Jugend* in 1910, they were quite different from the pen and ink work that made him famous.

This was the Heinrich Kley who was on record, but it was not the Heinrich Kley who was now pouring in sketches to *Jugend* and the great Munich humor periodical, *Simplizissimus.* Something had happened to him, but just what we do not know. The Heinrich Kley who had once "caught the poetry" of factories now revealed the Devil smirking behind smoke stacks; the Kley who had painted symbolically acceptable historical murals in city halls and post offices now daggered bureaucracy at every possible occasion. Kley had now become a "Rubens corrupted by Rabelais."

Kley now became a famous man, and it is easy enough to see why. Even beyond the technical virtuosity which his pen sketches show, he captured the disillusionment that was such a strong under-current in Germany (despite the war spirit which existed at other levels), and his jibes drew emotional resonance from his audience. He was a deft pricker of bubbles; even shocking in the expression of his perceptions. Social life, as illustrated by Kley, took on the quality of Restif de la Brettonne or Crebillon, and cruelty and pain and ironic laughter emerged unexpectedly in the jittery lines that crossed and intercrossed so individualistically.

Kley now started to divulge a world of metaphor and paradox as wildly bizarre as the visions of the elder Breughel or the animal scrolls of 13th century Japan, with both of which he has obvious affinities. Animals and monsters and weird emergences of bestiality from a human base all symbolized the various vices and follies that beset mankind: with virtues Kley had little concern.

At first glance we might think that Kley had some deep symbolism in mind, with his elephants, bird-women, satyrs, crocodiles, and assorted chimeras, but a closer examination shows that there are only a few elementary equations to be drawn: The following items, for example, are equal members of a long equation: elephants, babies and children, lubberliness, and coy, awkward innocence. (Elephants may have entered the equation because of their popularity in the advertising of his day.) Perhaps this equation is the reason that the picture of the elephant-seller arouses a feeling of horror and dismay in some viewers. Elsewhere, his symbolism is often traditional: the centaur usually equals lust, the faun or devil is usually to be found where human suffering is strong. Inversions of image are sometimes used, like racing snails, and puns and word and thought play find their place upon his paper. The erotic element is strong, and there is a certain infantile delight in words and utensils and postures suggestive of excretion—an obvious desire to shock at all costs.

As we glance back at these drawings from 1960, they now seem to be an integral part of the multi-channeled artistic outflow that was going on in Continental Europe in the 1910's and early 1920's. Kley lived in the same Munich that harbored Kandinsky, Klee, and the other Blue Riders. Yet despite coincidence in time and space, there seems to have been no social or artistic relationship between Kley and the modernists. Perhaps this was a difference of age: Kley was now about 50, paunchy and solemn, according to a self-portrait of this time. Perhaps it was because Kley was more absorbed with the world of pain and revulsion than they were. Perhaps Kley, an astonishing draftsman whose animal sketches rank technically among the best, had little understanding and sympathy for the experiments of men who were far beneath him in technique.

This was Heinrich Kley during his last period of productivity, between 1908 and World War I; a mysterious satirist and satyr, who seems to have felt pain where others laughed, and laughed, not always pleasantly, where others were silent. We know nothing about him personally, beyond what can be guessed from the strange reversal in his life and the personality that emerges from his work. After the appearance of his books (*Skizzenbuch* [1909], *Skizzenbuch II* [1910], *Sammel-Album* [1923], *Leut' und Viecher* [1912] he only occasionally illustrated art books. In the March 1939 issue of *Gebrauchsgraphik*, however, Kley is referred to as an outstanding contemporary commercial artist. The article reproduces a delicately colored industrial scene from the Krupp plant and some pen and ink sketches— in sketchbook style—which he had drawn for the Minimax catalogue for the year. After this he drops out of sight.

Kley's work was very popular for a time, and each of his books—which contain both periodical illustrations and new work—went through several editions. It is easy to understand, however, why he and his work would have been feared and disliked in the Germany that was emerging in the third and fourth decades of the century. He is ignored in histories of the magazines to which he contributed, and is passed over in silence in books on the art movements of Munich, although many men of lesser ability are discussed.

Kley's death has been reported many times, so that it is not certain just when he actually did die. A rumor of his death in the early 1940's has been denied. According to some authorities he died on August 2, 1945; according to others, he died on February 8, 1952. Kley, who perpetually evoked the demonic and absurd in man, would have enjoyed this confusion.

New York
November, 1960

Dover Publications, Inc.

SKETCHBOOK
SKIZZENBUCH

SKETCHBOOK
One Hundred Pen Drawings
by
HEINRICH KLEY

SKIZZENBUCH
Hundert Federzeichnungen
von
HEINRICH KLEY

Wet Nurse to Elephants
Die Elefantenamme

The Tip I
Das Trinkgeld I

The Tip II
Das Trinkgeld II

Springtime
Der Frühling

A Game of Diabolerina
Diaballeteuse

12

Love's Labor's Lost
Verlorene Liebesmüh

14

What a devilish stench!
Pfui Deifl!

15

Committee for Public Morals
Die Sittenkommission

16

Sabotage
Betriebsstörung

18

The pastor sleeps. The noontime meal
Was ample, and the day is hot.
And Karo too is stuffed from head to heel.
A comfort now prevails of sated glut.

But while the pastor's sleeping for the nonce
A dream approaches—horrid and abhorred:
That he was truly, all at once,
As poor as Jesus Christ, Our Lord.

Herr Pastor schläft. Das Mittagessen
War reichlich, und der Tag ist schwül.
Auch Karo hat sich vollgefressen.
Es herrscht ein sattes Wohlgefühl.

Indessen der Herr Pastor schliefe,
Kommt ihm ein Traum, der schrecklich ist:
Dass er mit einmal effektive
So arm sei wie Herr Jesus Christ.

Picnic
Picknick

The Ladies' Marching Band
Die Damenkapelle

24

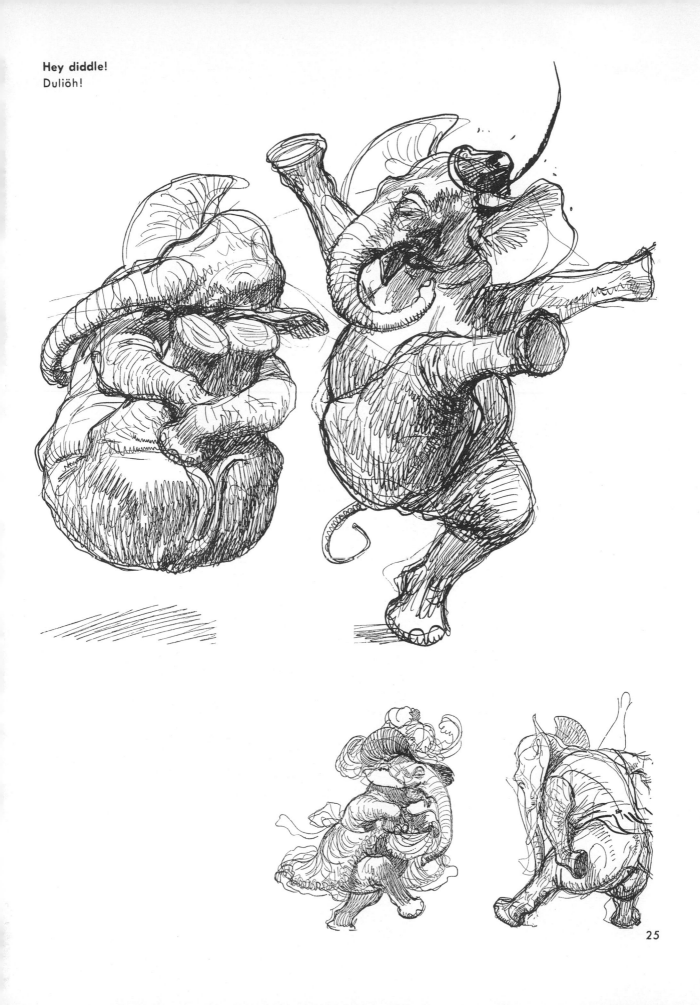

"And why shouldn't I play the guitar?"
"Warum soll denn ich nicht Guitarr spielen?"

"Sure I play the guitar. Now all the more!"
"Freilich spiel ich Guitarr. Jetzt erst recht!"

After the Ball
Nach dem Ball

Chamber Trio
Kammertrio

Visit of Condolence
Beileid

Accordion
Harmonika

The Breastwork
Die Brüstung

How Disgusting!
Igitt igitt!

Quartet I
Quartett I

Quartet II
Quartett II

Asking for Her Hand
Die Werbung

Red-faced Messenger Service, Inc.*
Rote Radler

*Rote Radler was a messenger service in Germany. The joke consists of the pun on *rot*, which means both red and red-faced.

Moving Day
Umzug

The Tenor
Der Tenor

41

The Airship
Das Luftschiff

43

When a boy and a girl are in accord before God and have their little toothbrushes along, the whole world is theirs.

Wenn zwei vor Gott sich einig sind und ihre Zahnbürstlen bei sich haben, gehört ihnen die ganze Welt.

44

Orient Express
Orient-Express

Solitude in the Royal Prussian Forest
Kgl. preuss. Waldeinsamkeit

*From top to bottom the signs on the tree read: "Keep out" (Betreten Verboten), "No Cars" (Befahren des Waldes Automobil), and "Society for Beautification" (Verschönerungsverein).

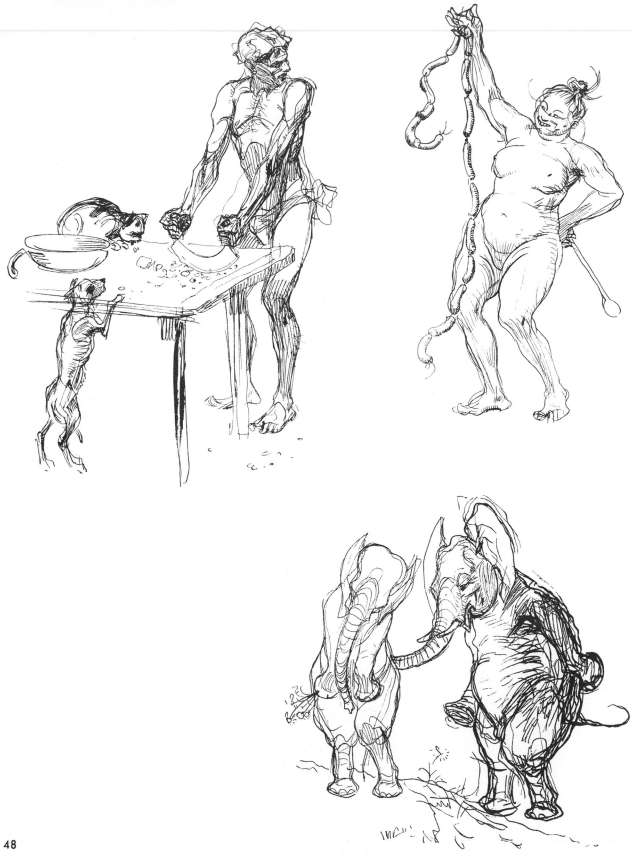

Away from Rome!
Los von Rom!

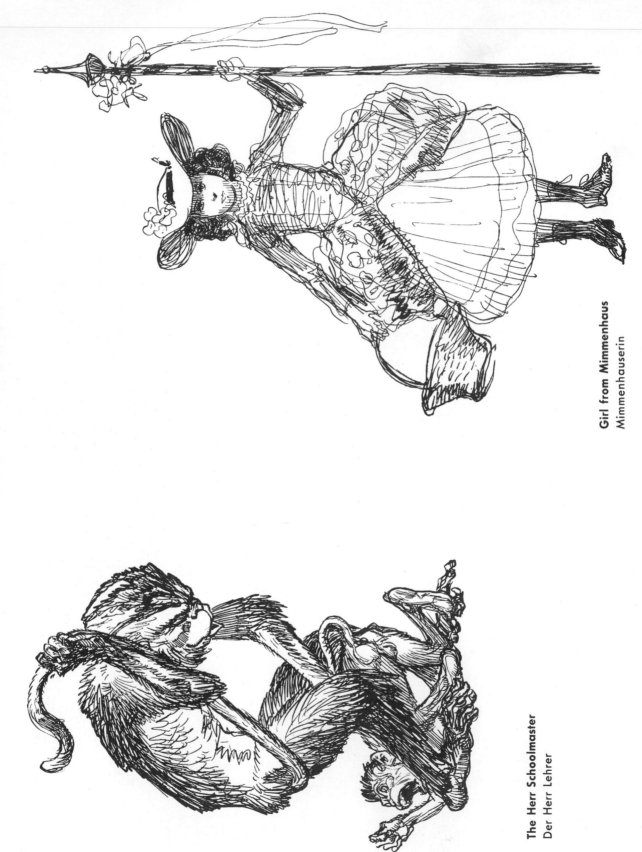

Girl from Mimmenhaus
Mimmenhauserin

The Herr Schoolmaster
Der Herr Lehrer

50

In Front of the Fireplace
Vor dem Kamin

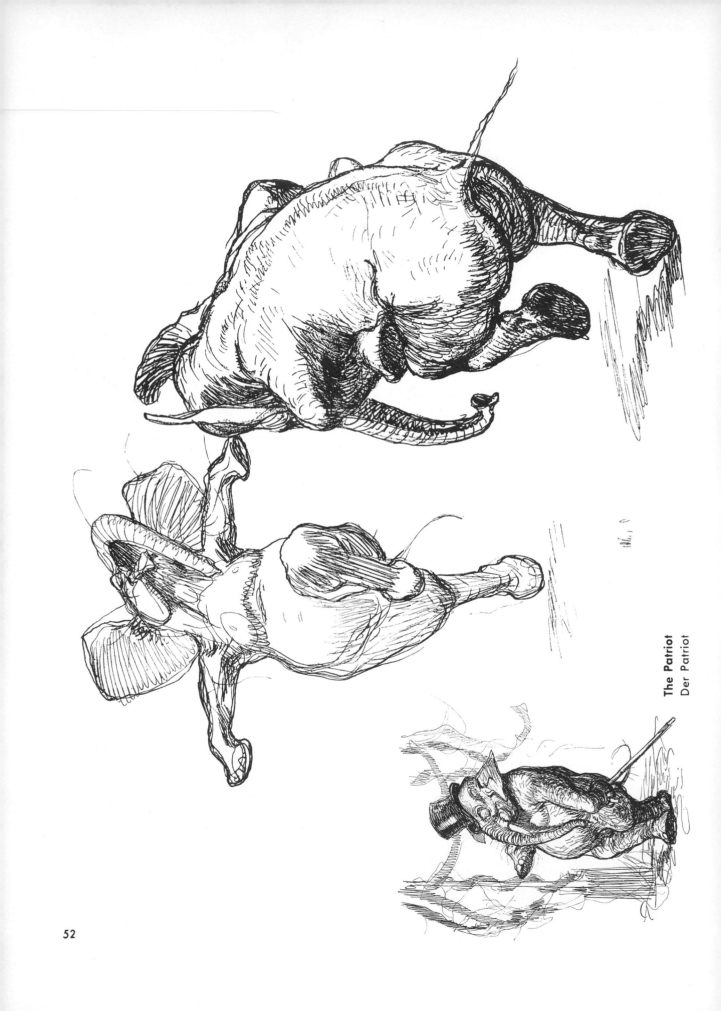

The Patriot
Der Patriot

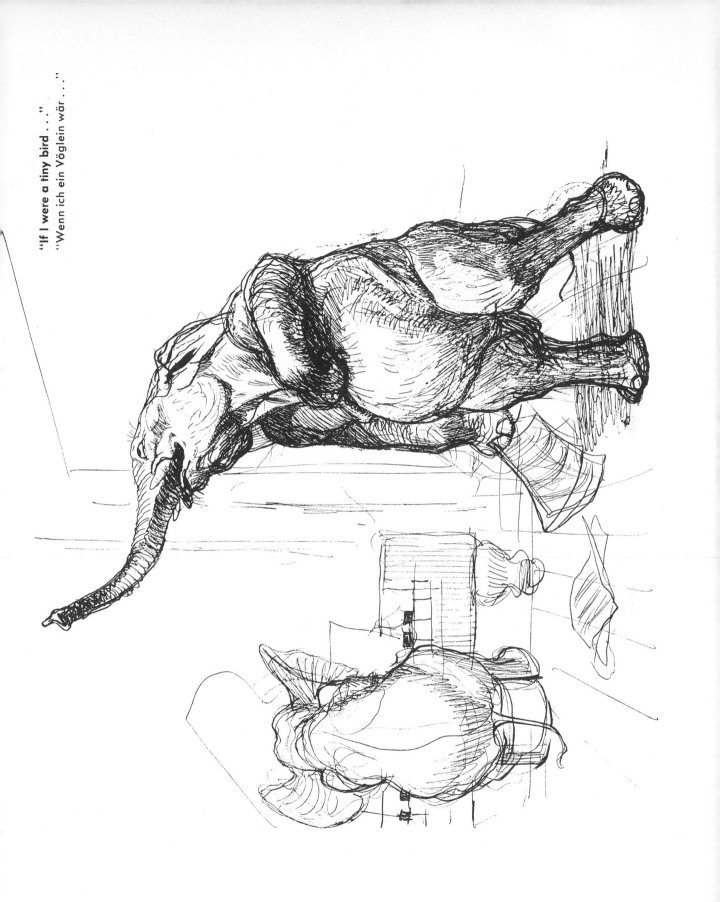

The Copyists
Die Kopisten

Idyll at the South Pole
Südpol-Idyll

A Love Story
Eine Liebesgeschichte

57

Doctor of Engineering
Dr. ing.

The Theater Director
Der Herr Direktor

62

SKETCHBOOK II
SKIZZENBUCH II

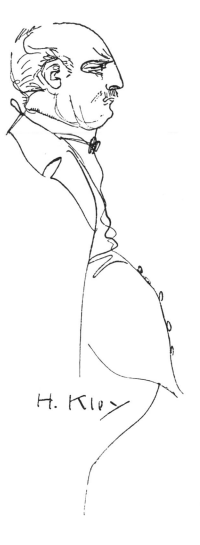

H. Kley

SKETCHBOOK II
One Hundred Pen Drawings
by
HEINRICH KLEY

SKIZZENBUCH II
Hundert Federzeichnungen
von
HEINRICH KLEY

Decorate Your Home!
Schmücke dein Heim!

The Nursemaid
Das Kindsmädchen

Mole and Purebred Pig
Maulwurf und Edelschwein

Carnival
Fasching

The Battle-tested Veteran
Der schlachterprobte Veteran

Bazaar Furies
Basarfurien

Auntie Tells a Fairy Tale
Märchentante

Parlor Game
Gesellschaftsspiel

75

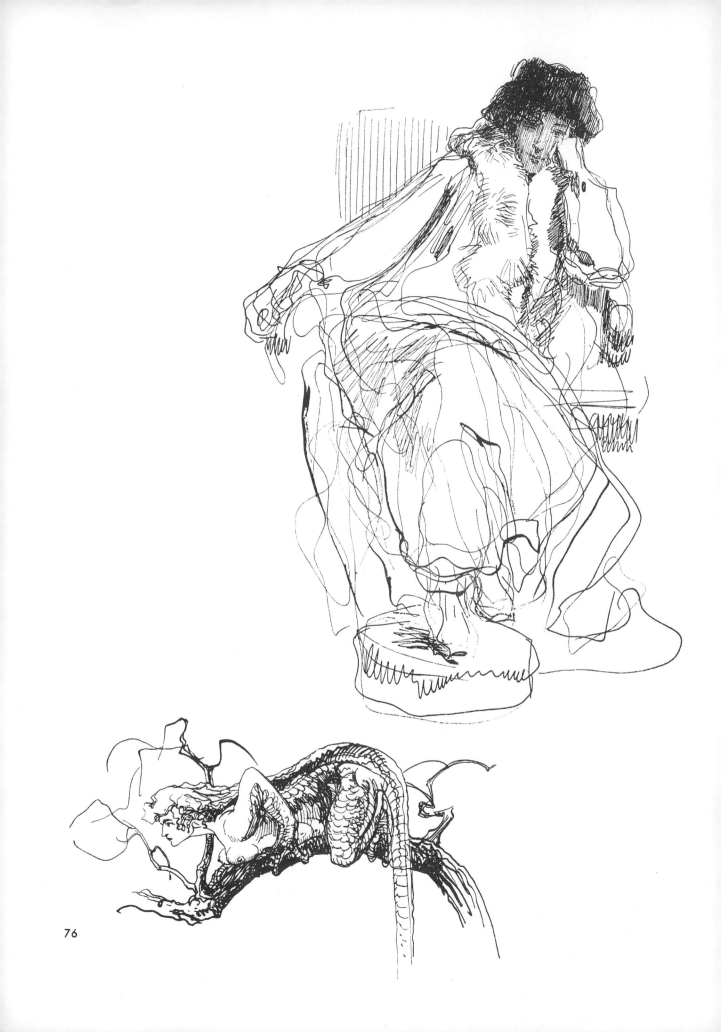

76

Business Is Bad
Schlechte Geschäfte

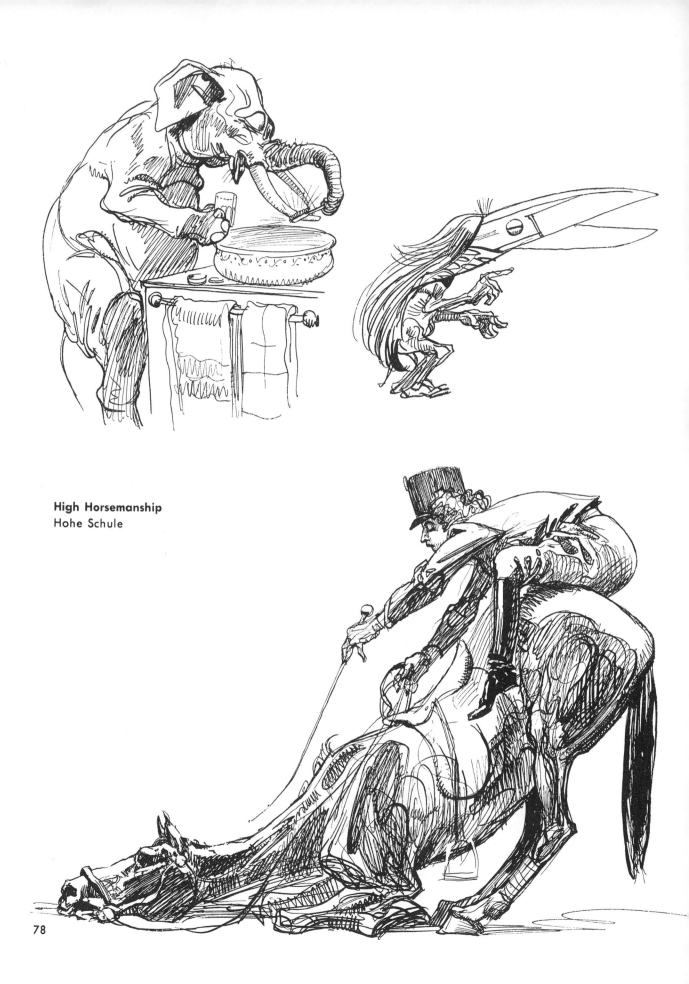

High Horsemanship
Hohe Schule

The Aesthete
Der Aesthet

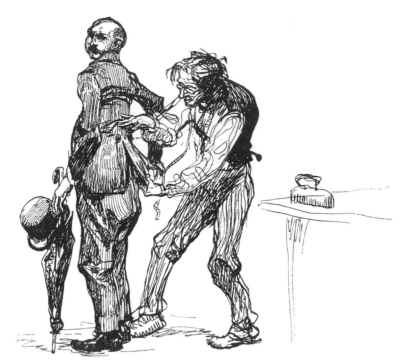

Almost Every Inch a Gentleman
Fast jeder Zoll ein Kavalier

Ballast
Ballast

Asylum for Cold-water Cures
Kaltwasserheilanstalt

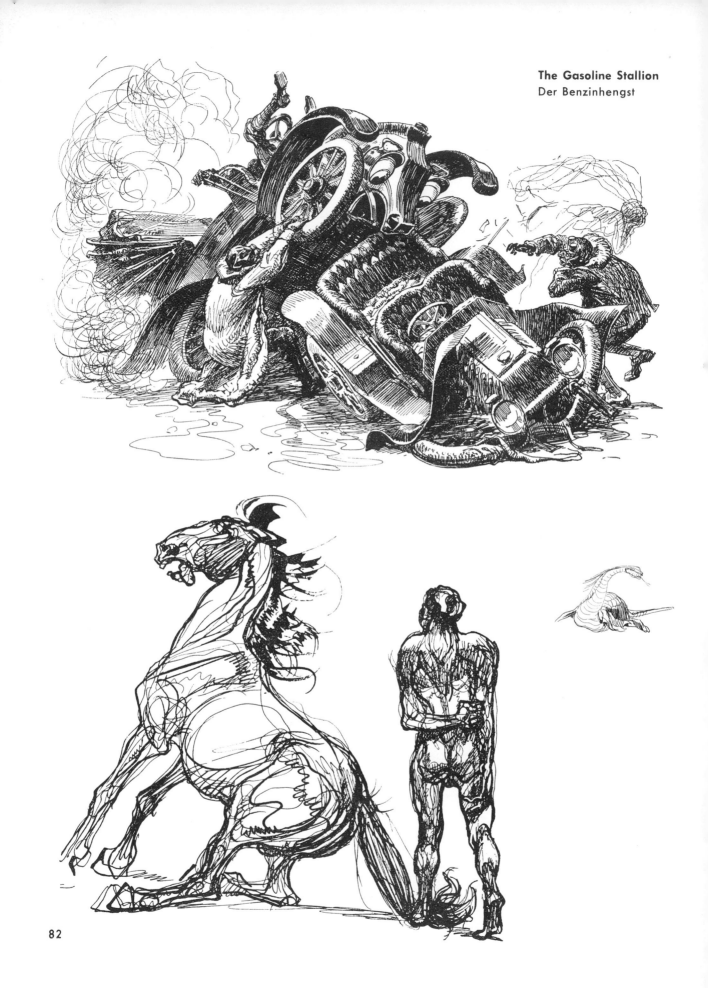

"Pardon me—how do I get to the YMCA?"
"Pardon—wie komm ich hier am nächsten zum
Vereinshaus christlicher junger Männer?"

Fruit Fair
Obsthandel

The Handstand
Der Handstand

84

Staying-power at Cards
Der Dauerskat

Bucolic Intermezzo
Schäferstündchen

Giant's Toy
Riesenspielzeug

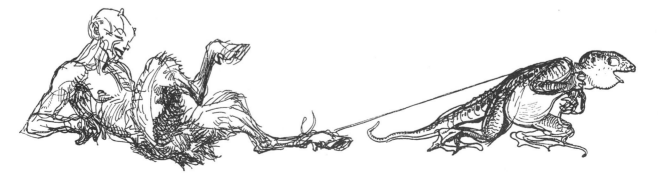

Popocatepetl
Popocatepetl*

*Popocatepetl is a volcano in Mexico.
†The sign on the figure reads, "Families can cook their coffee here."

Training
Training

Grand House Cleaning
Kehraus

Little Seesaw Man
Das Wagmännle

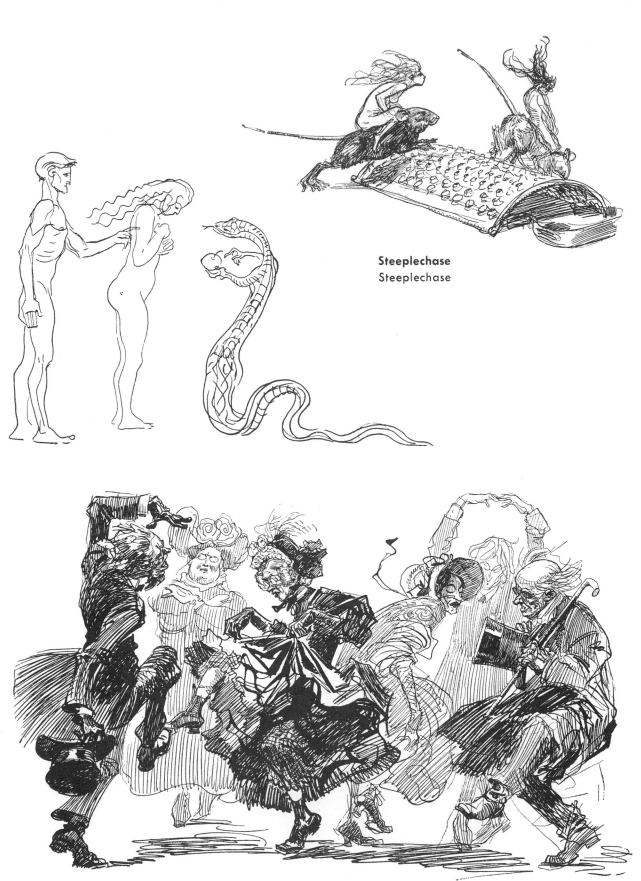

Steeplechase
Steeplechase

Grand Ball of the Diocese
Diözesanball

94

Human Shish Kebab
Menscherln à la fourchette

The End Hallows the Means
Der Zweck heiligt das Mittel

Tug of War
Tauziehen

*The sign above the door reads, "Marriage License Bureau."

The Traveller on a Pleasure Trip
Der Vergnügungsreisende

Final Spurt
Endspurt

The Navy Chaplain
Der Marinepfarrer

Caught in the Act
In flagranti

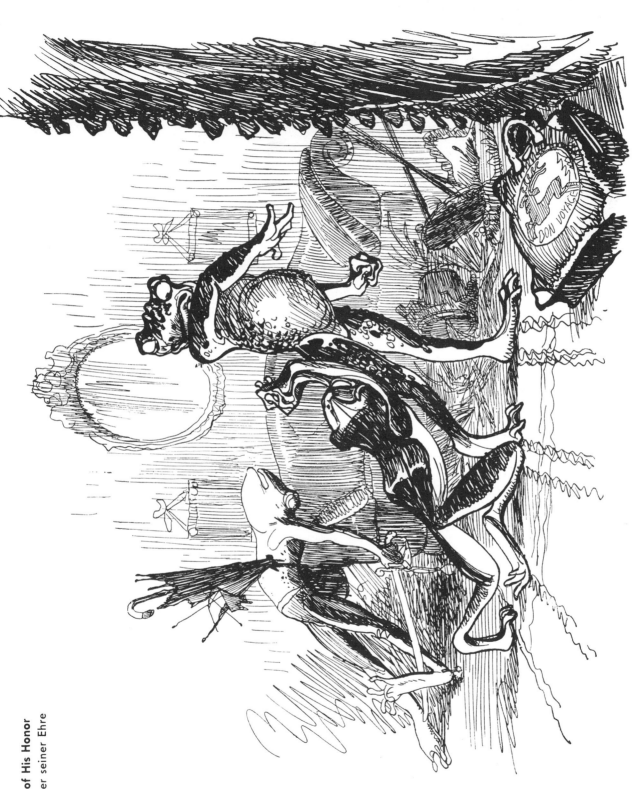

Avenger of His Honor
Der Rächer seiner Ehre

The Bridegroom
Der Bräutigam

The Bride
Die Braut

Tourist Season in Munich
Fremdensaison in München

On the Skating Rink
Auf der Eisbahn

Stoves with a Sweet Tooth
Naschende Oefen

*The sign above the cart reads, "V. Smirelli Ice Cream."

Ladies' Gym Group
Damenriege

Strike! All Nine Pins Are Down!
Alle Neune!

107

Cloudburst
Platzregen

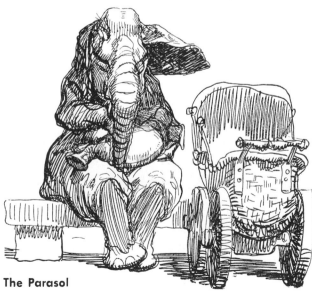

The Parasol
Der Sonnenschirm

Like Cures Like
*Similia similibus**

*The complete Latin expression is *Similia similibus curantur* (lit. Like [ailments] are cured by like.)

110

Girls at the Butter Churn
(Young Ladies at the Margarine Tub)

Mädlen am Butterfass
(Junge Damen an der Marjarintonne)

The Politicians
Die Politiker

Street Race
Strassenrennen

The Open Sandwich
Das belegte Brot

The Metaphysician
Der Metaphysiker

The Child Prodigy
Das Wunderkind

114

Mrs. Cook
Mrs. Cook

The Ivory Tusk
Das Elfenbein

*The sign above the door reads, "Municipal Pawn-shop" (Städtische Pfandleihe Anstalt).

How Shall I Tell My Child?
Wie sag ich's meinem Kinde?

Ju Jitsu
Dschiu Dschitsu

118

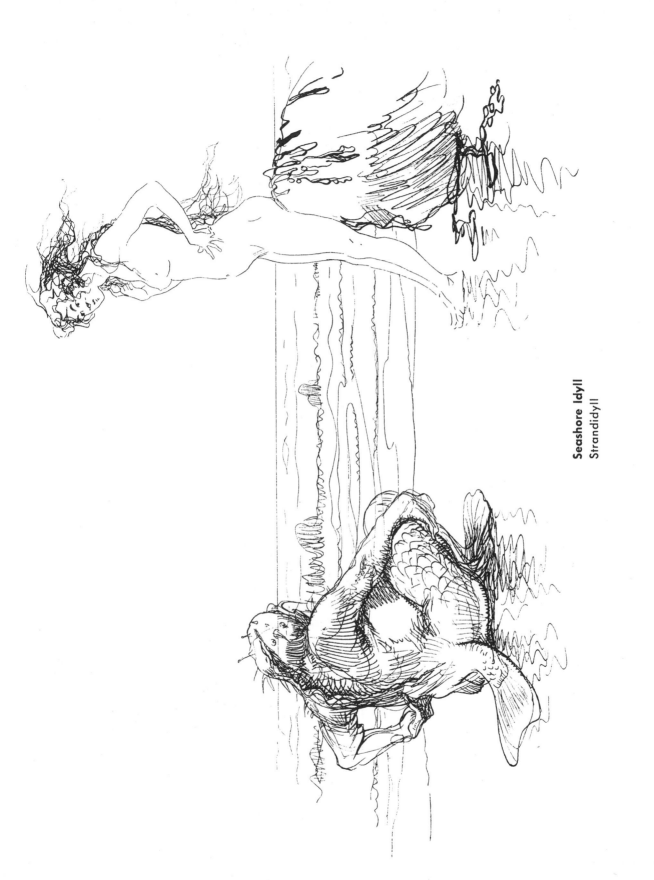

Seashore Idyll
Strandidyll

119

Getting a General, Well-rounded View
Allgemeine Rundschau*

Adagio
Adagio

Allgemeine Rundschau refers to a German periodical of that name. *Rundschau* can also mean an overall survey, in this case as afforded by a high-flying balloon.

The Train
Die Schleppe

121

England Victorious
England siegt

The Maiden's Prayer
Das Gebet der Jungfrau

Potiphar's Wife
Frau Potiphar

124

The Son-in-law
Der Schwiegersohn

Prayer Before the Battle
Gebet vor der Schlacht

125

The Finish at the Snails' Race
Schneckenfinish

Man, Made of Butter
Buttermensch

The Alpinist
Der Hochtourist

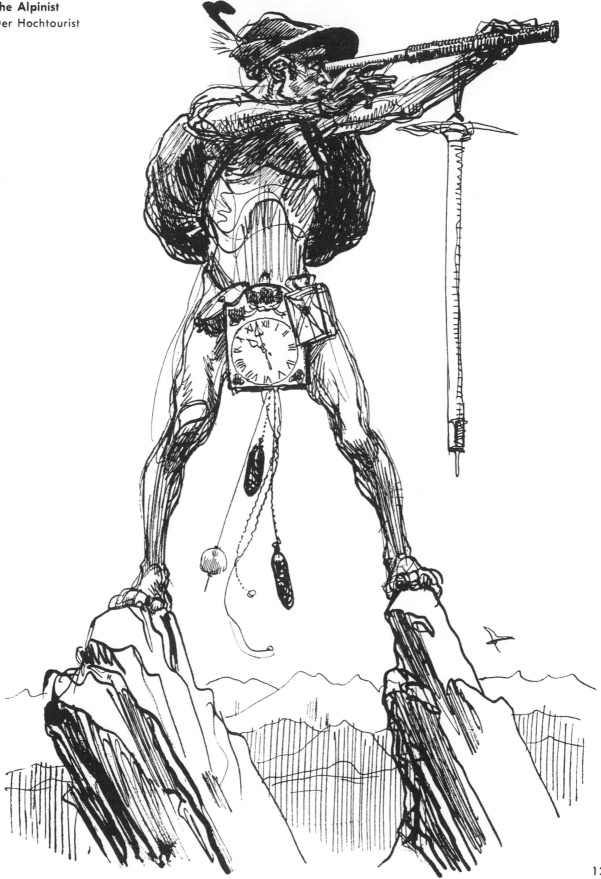

Dance Craze
Tanzpest

Aunt Mina
Tante Mina

Dover Books on Art

VASARI ON TECHNIQUE, G. Vasari. Pupil of Michelangelo, outstanding biographer of Renaissance artists reveals technical methods of his day. Marble, bronze, fresco painting, mosaics, engraving, stained glass, rustic ware, etc. Only English translation, extensively annotated by G. Baldwin Brown. 18 plates. 342pp. 5⅜ x 8. **T717 Paperbound $2.00**

FOOT-HIGH LETTERS: A GUIDE TO LETTERING, M. Price. 28 16″ x 22″ plates, give classic Roman alphabet, one foot high per letter, plus 9 other 2″-high letter forms for each letter. 16 page syllabus. Ideal for lettering classes, home study. 28 plates in box. **T239 $6.00**

A HANDBOOK OF WEAVES, G. H. Oelsner. Most complete book of weaves, fully explained, differentiated, illustrated. Plain weaves, irregular, double-stitched, filling satins; derivative, basket, rib weaves; steep, broken, herringbone, twills, lace, tricot, many others. Translated, revised by S. S. Dale; supplement on analysis of weaves. Bible for all handweavers. 1875 illustrations. 410pp. 6⅛ x 9¼. **T209 Clothbound $5.00**

JAPANESE HOMES AND THEIR SURROUNDINGS, E. S. Morse. Classic describes, analyses, illustrates all aspects of traditional Japanese home, from plan and structure to appointments, furniture, etc. Published in 1886, before Japanese architecture was contaminated by Western, this is strikingly modern in beautiful, functional approach to living. Indispensable to every architect, interior decorator, designer. 307 illustrations. Glossary. 410pp. 5⅝ x 8⅜. **T746 Paperbound $2.00**

DESIGN FOR ARTISTS AND CRAFTSMEN, L. Wolchonok. The most thorough course on the creation of art motifs and designs. Shows you step-by-step, with hundreds of examples and 113 detailed exercises, how to create original designs from geometric patterns, plants, birds, animals, humans, and man-made objects. "A great contribution to the field of design and crafts," N. Y. SOCIETY OF CRAFTSMEN. More than 1300 entirely new illustrations. xv + 207pp. 7⅞ x 10¾. **T274 Clothbound $4.95**

HANDBOOK OF DESIGNS AND DEVICES, C. P. Hornung. A remarkable working collection of 1836 basic designs and variations, all copyright-free. Variations of circle, line, cross, diamond, swastika, star, scroll, shield, many more. Notes on symbolism. "A necessity to every designer who would be original without having to labor heavily," ARTIST AND ADVERTISER. 204 plates. 240pp. 5⅜ x 8. **T125 Paperbound $1.90**

THE UNIVERSAL PENMAN, George Bickham. Exact reproduction of beautiful 18th century book of handwriting. 22 complete alphabets in finest English roundhand, other scripts, over 2000 elaborate flourishes, 122 calligraphic illustrations, etc. Material is copyright-free. "An essential part of any art library, and a book of permanent value," AMERICAN ARTIST. 212 plates. 224pp. 9 x 13¾. **T20 Clothbound $10.00**

THE CRAFTSMAN'S HANDBOOK, Cennino Cennini. The finest English translation of IL LIBRO DELL' ARTE, the 15th century introduction to art technique that is both a mirror of Quattrocento life and a source of many useful but nearly forgotten facets of the painter's art. 4 illustrations. xxvii + 142pp. D. V. Thompson, translator. 5⅜ x 8.   T54 Paperbound $1.25

THE BROWN DECADES, Lewis Mumford. A picture of the "buried renaissance" of the post-Civil War period, and the founding of modern architecture (Sullivan, Richardson, Root, Roebling), landscape development (Marsh, Olmstead, Eliot), and the graphic arts (Homer, Eakins, Ryder). 2nd revised, enlarged edition. Bibliography. 12 illustrations. xiv + 266 pp. 5⅜ x 8.
T200 Paperbound $1.65

THE HUMAN FIGURE, J. H. Vanderpoel. Not just a picture book, but a complete course by a famous figure artist. Extensive text, illustrated by 430 pencil and charcoal drawings of both male and female anatomy. 2nd enlarged edition. Foreword. 430 illus. 143pp. 6⅛ x 9¼.   T432 Paperbound $1.45

PINE FURNITURE OF EARLY NEW ENGLAND, R. H. Kettell. Over 400 illustrations, over 50 working drawings of early New England chairs, benches, beds, cupboards, mirrors, shelves, tables, other furniture esteemed for simple beauty and character. "Rich store of illustrations . . . emphasizes the individuality and varied design," ANTIQUES. 413 illustrations, 55 working drawings. 475pp. 8 x 10¾.   T145 Clothbound $10.00

BASIC BOOKBINDING, A. W. Lewis. Enables both beginners and experts to rebind old books or bind paperbacks in hard covers. Treats materials, tools; gives step-by-step instruction in how to collate a book, sew it, back it, make boards, etc. 261 illus. Appendices. 155pp. 5⅜ x 8.   T169 Paperbound $1.35

DESIGN MOTIFS OF ANCIENT MEXICO, J. Enciso. Nearly 90% of these 766 superb designs from Aztec, Olmec, Totonac, Maya, and Toltec origins are unobtainable elsewhere. Contains plumed serpents, wind gods, animals, demons, dancers, monsters, etc. Excellent applied design source. Originally $17.50. 766 illustrations, thousands of motifs. 192pp. 6⅛ x 9¼.
T84 Paperbound $1.85

HAWTHORNE ON PAINTING. Vivid re-creation, from students' notes, of instructions by Charles Hawthorne at Cape Cod School of Art. Essays, epigrammatic comments on color, form, seeing, techniques, etc. "Excellent," TIME. 100pp. 5⅜ x 8.
T653 Paperbound $1.00

BYZANTINE ART AND ARCHEOLOGY, O. M. Dalton. Still most thorough work in English on Byzantine art forms throughout ancient and medieval world. Analyzes hundreds of pieces, covers sculpture, painting, mosaic, jewelry, textiles, bronze, glass, etc. Historical development; specific examples; iconology and ideas; symbolism. A treasure-trove of material about one of most important art traditions, will supplement and expand any other book in area. Bibliography of over 2500 items. 457 illustrations. 747pp. 6⅛ x 9¼.   T776 Clothbound $7.50

HANDBOOK OF ORNAMENT, F. S. Meyer. One of the largest collections of copyright-free traditional art: over 3300 line cuts of Greek, Roman, Medieval, Renaissance, Baroque, 18th and 19th century art motifs (tracery, geometric elements, flower and animal motifs, etc.) and decorated objects (chairs, thrones, weapons, vases, jewelry, armor, etc.). Full text. 300 plates. 3300 illustrations. 562pp. 5⅜ x 8.   T302 Paperbound $2.25

THREE CLASSICS OF ITALIAN CALLIGRAPHY, Oscar Ogg, ed. Exact reproductions of three famous Renaissance calligraphic works: Arrighi's OPERINA and IL MODO, Tagliente's LO PRESENTE LIBRO, and Palatino's LIBRO NUOVO. More than 200 complete alphabets, thousands of lettered specimens, in Papal Chancery and other beautiful, ornate handwriting. Introduction. 245 plates. 282pp. 6⅛ x 9¼.   T212 Paperbound $1.95

FOUNDATIONS OF MODERN ART, A. Ozenfant. Stimulating discussion of human creativity from paleolithic cave painting to modern painting, architecture, decorative arts. Fully illustrated with works of Gris, Lipchitz, Léger, Picasso, primitive, modern artifacts, architecture, industrial art, much more. 226 illustrations. 368pp. 6⅛ x 9¼.   T215 Paperbound $1.95

METALWORK AND ENAMELLING, H. Maryon. Probably the best book ever written on the subject. Tells everything necessary for the home manufacture of jewelry, rings, ear pendants, bowls, etc. Covers materials, tools, soldering, filigree, setting stones, raising patterns, repoussé work, damascening, niello, cloisonné, polishing, assaying, casting, and dozens of other techniques. The best substitute for apprenticeship to a master metalworker. 363 photos and figures. 374pp. 5½ x 8½.

T183 Clothbound $8.00

SHAKER FURNITURE, E. D. and F. Andrews. The most illuminating study of Shaker furniture ever written. Covers chronology, craftsmanship, houses, shops, etc. Includes over 200 photographs of chairs, tables, clocks, beds, benches, etc. "Mr. & Mrs. Andrews know all there is to know about Shaker furniture," Mark Van Doren, NATION. 48 full-page plates. 192pp. 7⅞ x 10¾.   T679 Paperbound $2.00

AFRICAN SCULPTURE, Ladislas Segy. 163 full-page plates illustrating masks, fertility figures, ceremonial objects, etc., of 50 West and Central African tribes—95% never before illustrated. 34-page introduction to African sculpture. "Mr. Segy is one of its top authorities," NEW YORKER. 164 full-page photographic plates. Introduction. Bibliography. 244pp. 6⅛ x 9¼.

T396 Paperbound $2.00

CALLIGRAPHY, J. G. Schwandner. First reprinting in 200 years of this legendary book of beautiful handwriting. Over 300 ornamental initials, 12 complete calligraphic alphabets, over 150 ornate frames and panels, 75 calligraphic pictures of cherubs, stags, lions, etc., thousands of flourishes, scrolls, etc., by the greatest 18th century masters. All material can be copied or adapted without permission. Historical introduction. 158 full-page plates. 368pp. 9 x 13.   T475 Clothbound $10.00

ANIMALS IN MOTION, Eadweard Muybridge. The largest collection of animal action photos in print. 34 different animals (horses, mules, oxen, goats, camels, pigs, cats, lions, gnus, deer, monkeys, eagles—and 22 others) in 132 characteristic actions. All 3919 photographs are taken in series at speeds up to 1/1600th of a second, offering artists, biologists, cartoonists a remarkable opportunity to see exactly how an ostrich's head bobs when running, how a lion puts his foot down, how an elephant's knee bends, how a bird flaps his wings, thousands of other hard-to-catch details. "A really marvellous series of plates," NATURE. 380 full-page plates. Heavy glossy stock, reinforced binding with headbands. 7⅞ x 10¾.   T203 Clothbound $10.00

THE HUMAN FIGURE IN MOTION, Eadweard Muybridge. The largest collection in print of Muybridge's famous high-speed action photos. 4789 photographs in more than 500 action-strip-sequences (at shutter speeds up to 1/6000th of a second) illustrate men, women, children—mostly undraped—performing such actions as walking, running, getting up, lying down, carrying objects, throwing, etc. "An unparalleled dictionary of action for all artists," AMERICAN ARTIST. 390 full-page plates, with 4789 photographs. Heavy glossy stock, reinforced binding with headbands. 7⅞ x 10¾.   T204 Clothbound $10.00

THE BOOK OF SIGNS, R. Koch. 493 symbols—crosses, monograms, astrological, biological symbols, runes, etc.—from ancient manuscripts, cathedrals, coins, catacombs, pottery. May be reproduced permission-free. 493 illustrations by Fritz Kredel. 104pp. 6⅛ x 9¼.   T162 Paperbound $1.00

A HANDBOOK OF EARLY ADVERTISING ART, C. P. Hornung. The largest collection of copyright-free early advertising art ever compiled. Vol. I: 2,000 illustrations of animals, old automobiles, buildings, allegorical figures, fire engines, Indians, ships, trains, more than 33 other categories! Vol. II: Over 4,000 typographical specimens; 600 Roman, Gothic, Barnum, Old English faces; 630 ornamental type faces; hundreds of scrolls, initials, flourishes, etc. "A remarkable collection," PRINTERS' INK.

Vol. I: Pictorial Volume. Over 2000 illustrations. 256pp. 9 x 12.
                   T122 Clothbound $10.00

Vol. II: Typographical Volume. Over 4000 specimens. 319pp. 9 x 12.   T123 Clothbound $10.00

Two volume set, Clothbound, only $18.50

PRIMITIVE ART, Franz Boas. A great American anthropologist covers theory, technical virtuosity, styles, symbolism, patterns, etc. of primitive art. The more than 900 illustrations will interest artists, designers, craftworkers. Over 900 illustrations. 376pp. 5⅜ x 8.   T25 Paperbound $1.95

ON THE LAWS OF JAPANESE PAINTING, H. Bowie. The best possible substitute for lessons from an oriental master. Treats both spirit and technique; exercises for control of the brush; inks, brushes, colors; use of dots, lines to express whole moods, etc. 66 illus. 272 pp. 6⅛ x 9¼.   T30 Paperbound $1.95

AN ATLAS OF ANATOMY FOR ARTISTS, F. Schider. This standard work contains 189 full-page plates, more than 647 illustrations of all aspects of the human skeleton, musculature, cutaway portions of the body, each part of the anatomy, hand forms, eyelids, breasts, location of muscles under the flesh, etc. 59 plates illustrate how Michelangelo, da Vinci, Goya, 15 others, drew human anatomy. New 3rd edition enlarged by 52 new illustrations by Cloquet, Barcsay. "The standard reference tool," AMERICAN LIBRARY ASSOCIATION. "Excellent," AMERICAN ARTIST. 189 plates, 647 illustrations. xxvi + 192pp. 7⅞ x 10⅝.   T241 Clothbound $6.00

AN ATLAS OF ANIMAL ANATOMY FOR ARTISTS, W. Ellenberger, H. Baum, H. Dittrich. The largest, richest animal anatomy for artists in English. Form, musculature, tendons, bone structure, expression, detailed cross sections of head, other features, of the horse, lion, dog, cat, deer, seal, kangaroo, cow, bull, goat, monkey, hare, many other animals. "Highly recommended," DESIGN. Second, revised, enlarged edition with new plates from Cuvier, Stubbs, etc. 288 illustrations. 153pp. 11⅜ x 9.
                              T82 Clothbound $6.00

ANIMAL DRAWING: ANATOMY AND ACTION FOR ARTISTS, C. R. Knight. 158 studies, with full accompanying text, of such animals as the gorilla, bear, bison, dromedary, camel, vulture, pelican, iguana, shark, etc., by one of the greatest modern masters of animal drawing. Innumerable tips on how to get life expression into your work. "An excellent reference work," SAN FRANCISCO CHRONICLE. 158 illustrations. 156pp. 10½ x 8½.   T426 Paperbound $2.00

THE HISTORY AND TECHNIQUE OF LETTERING, A. Nesbitt. A thorough history of lettering from the ancient Egyptians to the present, and a 65-page course in lettering for artists. Every major development in lettering history is illustrated by a complete alphabet. Fully analyzes such masters as Caslon, Koch, Garamond, Jenson, and many more. 89 alphabets, 165 other specimens. 317pp. 7½ x 10½.   T427 Paperbound $2.00

LETTERING AND ALPHABETS, J. A. Cavanagh. An unabridged reissue of "Lettering," containing the full discussion, analysis, illustration of 89 basic hand lettering styles based on Caslon, Bodoni, Gothic, many other types. Hundreds of technical hints on construction, strokes, pens, brushes, etc. 89 alphabets, 72 lettered specimens, which may be reproduced permission-free. 121pp. 9¾ x 8.   T53 Paperbound $1.25

PRINCIPLES OF ART HISTORY, H. Wölfflin. This remarkably instructive work demonstrates the tremendous change in artistic conception from the 14th to the 18th centuries, by analyzing 164 works by Botticelli, Dürer, Hobbema, Holbein, Hals, Titian, Rembrandt, Vermeer, etc., and pointing out exactly what is meant by "baroque," "classic," "primitive," "picturesque," and other basic terms of art history and criticism. "A remarkable lesson in the art of seeing," SAT. REV. OF LITERATURE. Translated from the 7th German edition. 150 illus. 254pp. 6⅛ x 9¼.   T276 Paperbound $2.00

A DIDEROT PICTORIAL ENCYCLOPEDIA OF TRADES AND INDUSTRY. Manufacturing and the Technical Arts in Plates Selected from "L'Encyclopédie ou Dictionnaire Raisonné des Sciences, des Arts, et des Métiers," of Denis Diderot, edited with text by C. Gillispie. Over 2000 illustrations on 485 full-page plates. Magnificent 18th century engravings of men, women, and children working at such trades as milling flour, cheesemaking, charcoal burning, mining, silverplating, shoeing horses, making fine glass, printing, hundreds more, showing details of machinery, different steps in sequence, etc. A remarkable art work, but also the largest collection of working figures in print, copyright-free, for art directors, designers, etc. Two vols. 920pp. 9 x 12. Heavy library cloth.   T421 Two volume set $18.50

SILK SCREEN TECHNIQUES, J. Biegeleisen, M. Cohn. A practical step-by-step home course in one of the most versatile, least expensive graphic arts processes. How to build an inexpensive silk screen, prepare stencils, print, achieve special textures, use color, etc. Every step explained, diagrammed. 149 illustrations, 201pp. 6⅛ x 9¼.   T433 Paperbound $1.55

STICKS AND STONES, Lewis Mumford. An examination of forces influencing American architecture: the medieval tradition in early New England, the classical influence in Jefferson's time, the Brown Decades, the imperial façade, the machine age, etc. "A truly remarkable book," SAT. REV. OF LITERATURE. 2nd revised edition. 21 illus. xvii + 228pp. 5⅜ x 8.
                    T202 Paperbound $1.60

THE AUTOBIOGRAPHY OF AN IDEA, Louis Sullivan. The architect whom Frank Lloyd Wright called "the master" records the development of the theories that revolutionized America's skyline. 34 full-page plates of Sullivan's finest work. New introduction by R. M. Line. xiv + 335pp. 5⅜ x 8.
                    T281 Paperbound $1.85

THE MATERIALS AND TECHNIQUES OF MEDIEVAL PAINTING, D. V. Thompson. An invaluable study of carriers and grounds, binding media, pigments, metals used in painting, al fresco and al secco techniques, burnishing, etc. used by the medieval masters. Preface by Bernard Berenson. 239pp. 5⅜ x 8.
                    T327 Paperbound $1.85

ART ANATOMY, Dr. William Rimmer. One of the few books on art anatomy that are themselves works of art, this is a faithful reproduction (rearranged for handy use) of the extremely rare masterpiece of the famous 19th century anatomist, sculptor, and art teacher. Beautiful, clear line drawings show every part of the body—bony structure, muscles, features, etc. Unusual are the sections on falling bodies, foreshortenings, muscles in tension, grotesque personalities, and Rimmer's remarkable interpretation of emotions and personalities as expressed by facial features. It will supplement every other book on art anatomy you are likely to have. Reproduced clearer than the lithographic original (which sells for $500 on up on the rare book market.) Over 1,200 illustrations.
                    T908 Paperbound $2.00